MOUNTAINS

By Melissa Cole

BLACKBIRCH®
PRESS

THOMSON
San Diego • Detroit • New York • San Francisco • Cleveland • New Haven, Conn. • Waterville, Maine • London • Munich

THOMSON
GALE

For more information, contact
The Gale Group, Inc.
27500 Drake Rd.
Farmington Hills, MI 48331-3535
Or you can visit our Internet site at http://www.gale.com

LIBRARY OF CONGRESS CATALOGING-IN-PUBLICATION DATA

Cole, Melissa S.
  Mountain / by Melissa S. Cole.
    p. cm. — (Wild America habitats)
  Summary: Describes the topography, climate, and plant and animal life of mountains, as well as the interaction that humans have with them.
  Includes bibliographical references (p.   ).
  ISBN 1-56711-806-2 (hardback : alk. paper)
  1. Mountain ecology—Juvenile literature. [1. Mountains. 2. Mountain ecology. 3. Ecology.]   I. Title. II. Series: Wild America habitats series.
  QH541.5.M65C65 2003
  577.5'3—dc21   2002011726

Printed in China
10 9 8 7 6 5 4 3 2 1

Contents

Introduction

Rugged snow-capped mountains are one of the most challenging types of environment, or habitat, in which to live. The tops of mountains are often covered in snow, and the weather is usually cold and windy at high elevations. There is very little oxygen available for plants and animals. Because so few trees grow in high elevations, there is not much shelter for animals. The ground is rocky and difficult to cross. Over millions of years, though, plants and animals have adapted to living in this harsh habitat.

The thin air and cold, windy climate of snow-capped mountains provide a harsh habitat for the creatures that live there.

Where Are Mountains Found?

Mountains are usually found in long lines, called ranges. The Rocky Mountains stretch along the whole length of North America. Alaska is home to the tallest peak in North America—Mount McKinley, which is part of the Alaska Range and is 20,321 feet (6,195 m) above sea level. The Brooks Range is also in Alaska.

Other large mountain ranges are found across the United States. The Coastal Range runs along the Washington, Oregon, and California coasts. The Sierra Nevadas and Sierra Madres extend across Nevada and California. The Great Smoky Mountains sit high in Tennessee. The oldest range in North America —the Appalachian Mountains—stretches from Canada to central Alabama.

The Rocky Mountain Range runs the length of North America.

What Makes Mountains Unique?

Mountains vary in shape and size. Each range has its own look and altitude. The higher a plant or animal lives, the more it has to adapt to cold temperatures, wind, and damaging rays from the sun. Mountaintops are covered with a layer of snow and ice for most of the year. These layers of ice press together and form alpine glaciers (huge sheets of ice). Glaciers can be millions of years old. They slowly slide down mountainsides and leave behind rocks and patches of bare gravel.

Mountains have several different areas or zones. Climate, plant, and animal life vary with altitude. High altitude areas have less oxygen and tend to be colder. Lower slopes have conditions that are similar to those found in surrounding lowlands. Plants and animals adapt to the zone in which they find it easiest to survive.

Glaciers slowly move down mountains and shape the terrain.

How Do Plants Survive on Mountains?

Plants live in mountain zones in which they can best survive. The highest spot on a mountain is its peak. Peaks are usually covered with snow year round. Plants are unable to grow on snowy peaks. Peaks range between 6,000 to 13,000 feet (1,829 m to 3,963 m) high. The place where the snow ends is called the snowline. It is steep and windy, and the soil is thin and covered with a layer of fine gravel. The snowline depends on the climate where the mountain is found. In cold Alaska, the snowline is lower than in warmer states.

Lichens (pictured) and some mosses are the only plants that can survive the high mountain altitudes.

The area below the snowline is often called the lichen (lie-ken) zone. Lichens are made up of algae and fungi. Only lichens and a few species of mosses can survive at this altitude. Below the lichen zone, alpine wildflowers and low shrubs grow. Saxifrages are the most common plants found at this elevation. Their roots grow into rock cracks to help anchor them to the ground. The word saxifrage means "rock breaker."

More plants are able to survive at lower elevations. Alpine meadows are filled with grasses and wildflowers. Below these meadows, the climate is mild and trees can grow. Pines, firs, and spruces, which are commonly called conifers or evergreens, grow in mountain forests. The elevation where the treeline—where trees are able to grow— occurs depends on the climate of the area. Lichens, mosses, fungi, ferns, and berry bushes also grow in forests.

Geological History

It takes millions of years for mountains to form—the Appalachian Mountains are more than 230 million years old! Mountains form in areas where the Earth's crust pushes up through the surface. Rocks are squeezed together and forced upward.

Some mountains, such as Mount Saint Helens and Mount Rainier, are volcanoes. A volcano forms when hot gases, rocks, and lava below the Earth's surface burst through the ground.

Glaciers also affect how mountains form. Alpine glaciers press down on packed snow and create ice. Gravity pulls the ice down the mountainside. It grinds against rocks as it goes down the slope. Some rocks break away and become part of the moving glacier. They are later deposited farther down the mountain when the glacier melts. This motion can change a mountain's landscape significantly.

There are many kinds of animals that live in mountain habitats. Birds, large predators, goats, elk, and deer are some animals that live on mountains. Just like plants, animals live in different zones. Animals sometimes must move around to find food. They usually stay in the zone, though, that best suits their feeding needs.

Some species of birds fly near mountain peaks. They are mostly large birds such as bald eagles, golden eagles, and California condors. These birds can hover and glide—even in strong winds. They have sharp eyesight and can spot prey far below them. Ground birds such as ptarmigan (tar-mi-gan) and blue grouse live above alpine meadows. These birds feed on seeds and insects. Woodpeckers peck holes in tree trunks to search for insects.

Top: Golden eagles have strong wings that allow them to fly high up on windy mountain peaks. **Bottom:** Blue grouse spend time in the meadows low down on mountains.

Rocky mountain goats and bighorn sheep live on stony slopes below the snowline. They can climb straight up steep mountainsides and leap from rock to rock. They nibble on lichens, low-growing plants, and wildflowers that grow in rocky cracks. Mule deer and elk graze on grasses and wildflowers in alpine meadows during spring and summer. When it gets too cold, they move down the mountain to live in the forest. They spend winter feeding on lichens, tree bark, and dried leaves.

Small plant-eating animals called herbivores dig tunnels and live in burrows underground. Many chipmunks and ground squirrels live in forests and feed on seeds, pinecones, and bugs. Porcupines also live in the forest. They find shelter between tree roots or in hollow logs. They feed on pine needles and tree bark.

Mountain goats make their way up steep mountainsides to search for food.

11

Predators, such as wolverines, are fierce and eat other animals such as hares and young deer. Bobcats are small, powerful, and fast cats. They feed on hares and ptarmigan. Short-tailed weasels can easily slip into the burrows of small animals in search of prey.

Large predators, such as cougars and grizzly bears, also inhabit mountain forests. Cougars feed on mule deer, elk, mountain goats, bighorn sheep, hares, ground squirrels, and ptarmigan. In spring, grizzly bears feed on animals that were killed by avalanches and rockslides. They also tear up acres of alpine meadow with their long claws to get at juicy lily bulbs. In fall, they gorge themselves on ground squirrels and berries.

Wolverines are fierce mountain predators that prey on hares, birds, and other small animals.

Food Chain

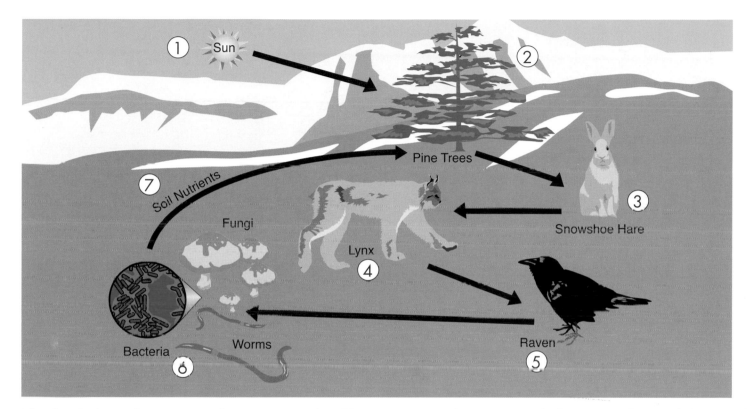

The food chain shows a step-by-step example of how energy in the mountain habitat is exchanged through food: The sun **(1)** is the first source of energy for all living things on earth. Green plants such as pine trees **(2)** are able to use sunlight and carbon dioxide in the air to create sugar, which the plants use as food. Snowshoe hares **(3)** eat green plants. In winter, when green plants are scarce, hares eat pine twigs, bark, and cones. Lynx feed on the hares **(4)**. When the lynx dies, its flesh becomes food for ravens **(5)** and other scavengers. Worms, fungi, bacteria, and other decomposers **(6)** feed on the rest of the lynx's body. Finally, these creatures or their waste products end up as soil nutrients **(7)**, which are then taken up by the roots of the pine trees and other plants as part of their nourishment. Then, the cycle repeats.

Climate

Earth's atmosphere acts like a blanket. It prevents heat from escaping into space. Gravity holds most of this blanket close to the Earth's surface. The atmosphere above mountain peaks (6,000 feet/1,829 m and higher) is very thin. This means there is less oxygen. Thin air lets in more damaging sun rays and also means that there is less carbon dioxide for plants to use.

Without a thick atmosphere to block the sun, daytime air temperatures can rise quite high in the mountains before plunging at night. Temperatures on mountains drop rapidly, especially at night when the sun is no longer out. The temperature falls by about 34°F/1°C every 650 feet (198 m) so mountain peaks can be as cold and windswept as the Arctic. At high altitudes, storms are frequent, and there are often strong winds. Winds can cause rockslides and avalanches. These conditions make living in a mountain habitat challenging for animals.

Thin air makes for freezing nighttime temperatures on mountain peaks.

Mount Rainier

Mount Rainier is in Washington. It is an active volcano. Mount Rainier is 14,410 feet (4,393 m) high. Its peak is covered with more than 35 square miles (91 square km) of snow and ice. In 1899, the 235,000 acres (951 square km) of land that surround Mount Rainier was established as a national park.

Life is especially hard for mountain animals in winter. Temperatures can drop below freezing. Strong winds may whip away an animal's body heat. Many animals grow thick coats to keep them warm during fall and winter. Some animals have a long, coarse outer layer of fur and a soft, downy undercoat to keep out the elements. This inner layer traps warm air next to an animal's skin. Mountain animals shed their fur to keep from overheating during summer.

Mountain goats have thick, white wool coats that keep them warm and hidden from predators on snowy mountaintops.

It is difficult to travel across icy rocks and deep, snowy mountain slopes. Mountain goats and bighorn sheep have hooves with narrow edges that dig into cracks in the rocks. They have special pads below their hooves. These rough pads allow them to climb straight up steep rock faces or to leap between rocks. Their flexible hooves have a split down the center that forms two toes. These toes spread out when they land, making it easier for them to balance.

Alpine marmots, chipmunks, ground squirrels, and grizzly bears sleep through winter. Their body temperatures drop and their heartbeats slow down. This deep sleep is called hibernation. It allows these animals to survive the harsh winter months without food until they wake up in the spring.

Top: Mountain goats' feet are ideal for climbing steep, rocky passes. Bottom: Ground squirrels have camouflaged coats that help them hide from predators.

Animals that live near the tops of mountains have very few trees to shelter them from other animals. To avoid predators, ptarmigan and snowshoe hares turn white in winter. Predators cannot see the white animals against the snow. In spring, the animals turn from white to grayish-brown. This makes them blend in with rocks. It is another way to hide and to keep from being eaten.

Marmots live in groups called colonies. They dig tunnels and burrows below the ground to avoid being eaten. When marmots leave their burrows to feed, several of them stand on high rocks to watch for predators. If a marmot senses danger, it makes a whistling sound. Colony members know to run to their burrows when they hear this sound.

Snowshoe hares have large furry feet and white fur. These traits allow them to race over the snow almost unseen by predators.

The food that animals eat in mountain habitats is often determined by the seasons. Many animals are killed in winter by rock-slides and avalanches—they will stay where they fell until spring. Predators patrol bases of rocky areas to feed on these dead animals in spring months when snow melts.

Other animals spend a lot of time preparing for lean winter months. Pikas collect grass and other plants to store until winter. They carry bundles of plants to rocks and lay them out to dry. In fall, pikas gather berries, twigs, leaves, thistles, and pine needles. A pika stands guard while its food dries to make sure that other pikas do not steal it. All of this dried plant material is kept in a burrow. This ensures pikas will have plenty to eat during cold winter months.

Pikas store up grass and other food in their burrows to eat over the long winter.

How Plants Adapt to Mountain Life

Most mountain plants grow close to the ground in clumps. This keeps them out of the wind. Many plants have dark leaves with hair on them. Dark colors soak up warmth faster than light colors do. The hair helps to hold heat in and protect them from the cold.

The mountain growing season is only 4 to 6 weeks long. Alpine wildflowers have adapted to this short growing season. They grow quickly and produce flowers and seeds within a matter of weeks.

Conifers, or evergreen trees, are well suited to cold weather. Their needles are tough so they continue to grow in winter. Seeds are protected within a hard cone called a pinecone. Conifer trees are shaped so that heavy snow can slide off their branches without breaking them.

Inset: Plants such as the lupine have adapted to cold mountain climates by growing dark, fuzzy leaves that hold in warmth. **Right:** Hardy conifers are shaped to shed snow buildup on their branches.

Humans and Mountains

Mountains are popular places for tourists to visit. Tourism has had some negative effects on mountain habitats, though. Towns and resorts have caused many species of plants and animals to move elsewhere or die.

Many mountain forests have been clear-cut (meaning all trees in a certain area are cut down). Tree roots that hold soil in place are removed during this process. Loose soil washes away when it rains. Without the nutrient-rich layer of topsoil, it is difficult for new trees and plants to grow.

Global warming is another worldwide concern. Gases such as carbon dioxide released from cars build up in the atmosphere and trap too much heat. If the world temperature increases too much and alpine glaciers melt, major flooding will occur.

There are ways to decrease the impact of global warming, though. People can help decrease the amount of carbon dioxide released into the environment by driving cars less and by using wind and solar power.

Mountain resorts are popular vacation spots, but they can upset the delicate mountain ecology.

A Mountain's Food Web

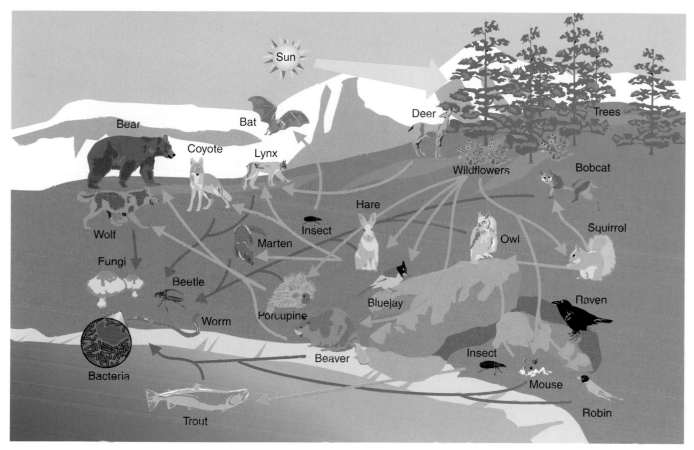

A food web shows how creatures in the habitat depend on one another to survive. The arrows in this drawing show the flow of energy from one creature to another in the mountain food web. Yellow arrows: creatures nourished by the sun; Green arrows: animals that eat the green plants for energy; Orange arrows: predators; Red arrows: scavengers and decomposers. From them, the energy returns to the soil and is taken up by green plants, and the cycle repeats.

Glossary

Adapt To change behavior or characteristics to increase chances of survival in a particular habitat

Alpine Meadows Areas below rocky mountain slopes that have grasses and wildflowers growing in them

Burrow A hole in the ground made by an animal for shelter

Decomposers Animals, such as earthworms, and plants, such as fungi, that eat dead tissue and return nutrients to the soil

Food Chain The process of energy passing between organisms as they feed upon one another

Food Web A series of food chains that are linked together

Glacier A moving sheet or river of ice that slowly slides down mountain slopes

Habitat The area in which a plant or animal naturally lives. Habitats provide living organisms with everything they need to survive—food, water, and shelter.

Herbivores Animals, such as mountain goats and pikas, that get their food and energy by eating plants

Hibernation A deep sleep or slowing down of bodily processes that allows an animal to survive through long winter periods

Lichen A type of organism formed by fungi and algae that live together

Predators Animals, such as cougars, that hunt other animals for food

Prey An animal killed and eaten by another animal

Scavengers Animals, such as ravens, that feed on animals that are already dead

For Further Reading

Books

Kehoe, Stacia Ward. *I Live in the Mountains.* New York: Powerkids Press, 2000.

Landau, Elaine. *Mountain Mammals.* New York: Childrens Press, 1996.

Pipes, Rose. *Mountains and Volcanoes.* Austin, TX: Raintree Steck-Vaughn, 1998.

Rauzon, Mark J. *Golden Eagles of Devil Mountain.* New York: Grolier, 2000.

Websites

Arctic National Wildlife Refuge site/Alaska Range, Brooks Range
www.anwr.org
Peakware/Appalachian Mountain site
www.peakware.com/encyclopedia/ranges/appalachian.htm
Rocky Mountain site
www.nps.ga/romo

Index